X-TREME FACTS: ENGINEERING

BRIDGES

by Catherine C. Finan

Minneapolis, Minnesota

Credits:
Cover and title page, Joachim Huber/Creative Commons; 4 top, Stanislav71/Shutterstock; 4 top left, 4 top right, Gorodenkoff/Shutterstock; 4 bottom, Morphart Creation/Shutterstock; 5 top, GrAl/Shutterstock; 5 top middle, Kues/Shutterstock; 5 middle, Golden Pixels LLC/Shutterstock; 5 middle background, MNXANL/Creative Commons; 5 bottom, u photostock/Shutterstock.com; 5 bottom right, Asier Romero/Shutterstock; 6 top, Peter James Platt, photographer/Titanium Motion Pictures/Public Domain; 6 bottom left, Hike The World/Shutterstock; 6 right, Pi.1415926535/Creative Commons; 7 top, Sion Hannuna/Shutterstock; 7 bottom, Henk Monster/Creative Commons; 7 bottom left, Andrey Arkusha/Shutterstock.com; 7 bottom right, orn340 Studio Images/Shutterstock; 8 top, Siyuwj/Creative Commons; 8–9 bottom, Martin Falbisoner/Creative Commons; 8 bottom right, Photo courtesy of Rutahsa Adventures/Creative Commons; 9 top, Bernard Gagnon/Creative Commons; 9 top left, Brocreative/Shutterstock; 9 top right, GOLFX/Shutterstock; 9 bottom right, Ysbrand Cosijn/Shutterstock; 10 top, PJMarriott/Creative Commons; 10 bottom, Krzysztof Golik/Creative Commons; 10 bottom right, Gino Santa Maria/Shutterstock; 11 top, Javier Casado Tirado/Creative Commons; 11 middle, Felver Alfonzo/Creative Commons; 11 bottom left, Gelpi/Shutterstock; 11 bottom, Joanbanjo/Creative Commons; 12 top, Paolo Trabattoni/Creative Commons; 12 bottom, Amfeli/Creative Commons; 12 bottom left, Lagui/Creative Commons; 12 bottom right, meunierd/Shutterstock; 13 top, Famartin/Creative Commons; 13 top left, Paul Michael Hughes/Shutterstock; 13 bottom, Glabb/Creative Commons; 13 bottom right, Creativa Images/Shutterstock; 14 top, Gavin Zeigler /Alamy; 14 top left, Tatyana Vyc/Shutterstock; 14 top right, 15 bottom right, 25 bottom right, LightField Studios/Shutterstock; 14 middle, Randy Hergenrether/Shutterstock; 14–15 bottom, Chuck Wagner/Shutterstock; 15 top SnvvSnvvSnvv/Shutterstock; 15 bottom, Mark Runde/Shutterstock; 16 top, William Strickland/Public Domain; 16 bottom, Christos Siatos/Shutterstock; 16 bottom left, Dragon Images/Shutterstock; 16 bottom right, Nanette Dreyer/Shutterstock; 17 top, Fred222wiki/Creative Commons; 17 top middle, taviphoto/Shutterstock.com; 17 top right, gift of Paul Roebling/Public Domain; 17 bottom, Tysto/Creative Commons; 17 bottom left, Jeka/Shutterstock; 18 top, CucombreLibre/Creative Commons; 18 middle, US National Park Service/Public Domain; 18 bottom, National Archives and Records Administration/Public Domain; 19 top, Prelinger Archives/Public Domain; 19 middle, Keep Smiling Photography/Shutterstock.com; 19 bottom, Bildagentur Zoonar GmbH/Shutterstock; 19 bottom left, 19 bottom right, Oqbas/Shutterstock; 20 top, University of Washington Libraries. Digital Collections/Public Domain; 20 middle, 21 top, 21 bottom, Stillman Fires Collection; Tacoma Fire Department/Public Domain; 20 bottom, Anatoliy Karlyuk/Shutterstock; 21 top left, 21 top right, LightField Studios/Shutterstock; 22 top, Aon_Skynotlimit/Shutterstock.com; 22 top right, Dalton Dingelstad/Shutterstock; 22 bottom, Zairon/Creative Commons; 23 top, John J Brown/Shutterstock; 23 top left, ViDI Studio/Shutterstock; 23 middle right, Barbara Carr/Boat sailing under the Williamsburg Bridge/CC BY-SA 2.0; 23 middle left, Saeed Majidi/Creative Commons; 23 bottom, 23 bottom left, Christophe95/Creative Commons; 24 top, Bear-Fotos/Shutterstock; 24 middle, Michel Rathwell/Creative Commons; 24–25 bottom, Joe Mabel/Creative Commons; 25 top left, Jan Drewes/Creative Commons; 25 top right, Tony Hisgett/Creative Commons; 25 top middle, Dietmar Rabich/CC BY-SA 4.0;26 top, Wut_Moppie/Shutterstock.com; 26 top right, Kuznetsov Dmitriy/Shutterstock; 26 bottom, BAZA Production/Shutterstock; 27 top, John Penney/Shutterstock.com; 27 top right, Prostock-studio/Shutterstock; 27 bottom, Kars Alfrink/Creative Commons; 27 bottom left, Bachkova Natalia/Shutterstock;/Creative Commons; 28 top left, MTKirk/Creative Commons; 28 bottom, Photo courtesy of Rutahsa Adventures/Creative Commons; 28–29, Austen Photography

Bearport Publishing Company Product Development Team
President: Jen Jenson; Director of Product Development: Spencer Brinker; Senior Editor: Allison Juda; Editor: Charly Haley; Associate Editor: Naomi Reich; Senior Designer: Colin O'Dea; Associate Designer: Elena Klinkner; Product Development Assistant: Anita Stasson

Produced for Bearport Publishing by BlueAppleWorks Inc.
Managing Editor for BlueAppleWorks: Melissa McClellan
Art Director: T.J. Choleva
Photo Research: Jane Reid

Library of Congress Cataloging-in-Publication Data is available at www.loc.gov or upon request from the publisher.

ISBN: 979-8-88509-164-0 (hardcover)
ISBN: 979-8-88509-171-8 (paperback)
ISBN: 979-8-88509-178-7 (ebook)

Copyright © 2023 Bearport Publishing Company. All rights reserved. No part of this publication may be reproduced in whole or in part, stored in any retrieval system, or transmitted in any form or by any means, electronic, mechanical, photocopying, recording, or otherwise, without written permission from the publisher.

For more information, write to Bearport Publishing, 5357 Penn Avenue South, Minneapolis, MN 55419.
Printed in the United States of America.

Contents

Take Me to the Bridge! ... 4
Different Styles ... 6
Now, That's Old! ... 8
Amazing Aqueducts ... 10
Awesome Arches ... 12
Cool Beams! ... 14
In Suspense! ... 16
The Great Golden Gate ... 18
A Big Bridge Blunder ... 20
Artsy Bridges ... 22
Bridge MVPs ... 24
A Bridge to the Future ... 26

Suspension Bridge ... 28
Glossary ... 30
Read More ... 31
Learn More Online ... 31
Index ... 32
About the Author ... 32

Take Me to the Bridge!

Every day, people travel on bridges without even thinking about it. Bridges cross over roads, rivers, and much more. From little walking bridges to huge highway bridges, these structures are everywhere! Although bridges may seem ordinary, they are actually incredible feats of **engineering**. Without them, we'd have to travel longer and farther to safely get from place to place. Let's cross that bridge and learn more . . .

People built the earliest bridges **by placing logs and stones across rivers and streams.**

HEY, THAT DOESN'T LOOK LIKE A REAL BRIDGE.

IT MAY BE SIMPLE, BUT IT'LL GET THE JOB DONE!

I'M OLD, BUT I'VE STILL GOT IT!

The ancient Romans built Caravan Bridge in Turkey about 3,000 years ago. It's still used today!

Different Styles

Ever since the first stepping-stones were used to cross streams, people have been looking to improve their bridge-building methods and designs. Some styles have stood the test of time. From ancient beam and arch bridges to modern suspension bridges, engineers have found incredible ways to get across difficult spaces. Let's check out some different kinds of bridges!

A beam bridge is a straight, horizontal structure supported by **piers**.

THIS OLD BRIDGE IS A GREAT WAY TO GO!

HEY! WHO ARE YOU CALLING OLD?!

Beam bridges are the oldest kind of bridge. Other bridges are similar in style, but they have more supports.

Truss bridges are supported by triangular-shaped bars.

Arch bridges have curved arches for support.

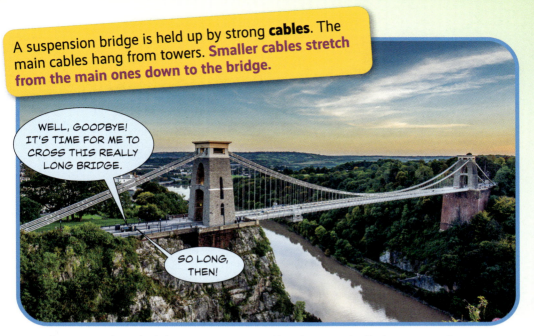

A suspension bridge is held up by strong **cables**. The main cables hang from towers. Smaller cables stretch from the main ones down to the bridge.

Suspension bridges can **span** the longest distances of any kind of bridge.

Cable-stayed bridges are also supported by cables. These supports run between the bridge's **deck** and its towers.

Now, That's Old!

It's not just bridge styles that have stood the test of time—many of the *actual bridges* built long ago are still standing! Greece's Arkadiko Bridge, built 3,200 years ago, is one of the oldest arch bridges in the world. A bridge in Rome, Italy, is more than 2,000 years old, and it's still used by thousands of people every day. China's oldest working bridge, Anji Bridge, was built 1,400 years ago. That's some strong engineering!

Anji Bridge got its name from a **Chinese word that means safe crossing.**

YOU'RE SAFE WITH ME!

The Inca people of Peru built a long grass bridge called Q'eswachaka 500 years ago. You can still walk across it today!

CROSSING THIS BRIDGE NEVER GETS OLD.

The Shaharah Bridge in Yemen was built in the 1600s. A **legend** says it was made to be destroyed quickly if enemies tried to cross it.

DO YOU THINK IT'S OKAY TO CROSS THAT BRIDGE?

I THINK SO! WE'RE NOT ANYONE'S ENEMIES!

Rialto Bridge in Venice, Italy, was completed in 1591. People still cross it today.

The famous **Renaissance** artist Michelangelo offered to design Rialto Bridge, but he was turned down!

WHAT A NICE BRIDGE!

LOOKS GOOD, BUT I COULD HAVE DONE BETTER.

Amazing Aqueducts

Bridges can do more than help people get from place to place. The ancient Romans built huge bridges called **aqueducts** to carry water from far away into towns and cities. They constructed the famous Pont du Gard aqueduct in France 2,000 years ago—and it still stands! What else can we learn about aqueducts?

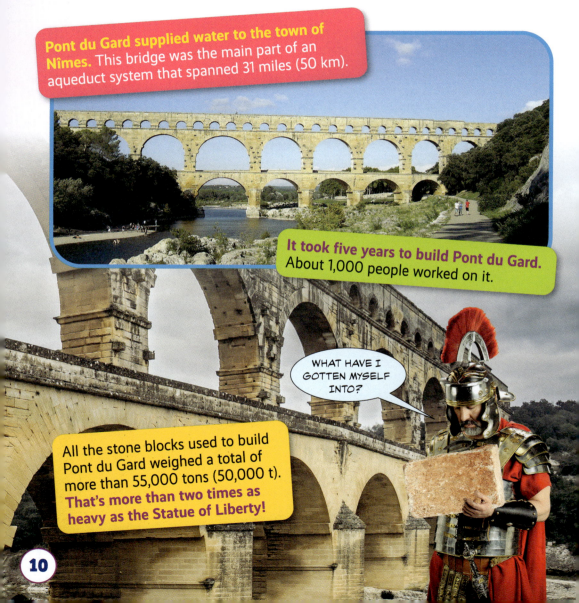

Pont du Gard supplied water to the town of Nîmes. This bridge was the main part of an aqueduct system that spanned 31 miles (50 km).

It took five years to build Pont du Gard. About 1,000 people worked on it.

WHAT HAVE I GOTTEN MYSELF INTO?

All the stone blocks used to build Pont du Gard weighed a total of more than 55,000 tons (50,000 t). That's more than two times as heavy as the Statue of Liberty!

Awesome Arches

The ancient Roman aqueducts were arch bridges. In fact, it was the Romans who first made arch bridges. This engineering feat allowed them to build much larger structures. An arch bridge is strong and stable because the arches carry the bridge's weight to the piers on each end. Arches are awesome!

Arch bridges were the first large bridges built to last a long time.

The ancient Romans built more than 930 stone arch bridges throughout Europe, Asia, and North Africa. **Many are still standing today!**

WOW! WE MUST'VE DONE SOMETHING RIGHT ALL THOSE YEARS AGO.

LOOK, OUR BRIDGE IS STILL HERE!

The Romans built all these bridges to make travel easier for their army.

12

Arch bridges are still built today. Instead of stone, they're made of steel, iron, and **concrete**.

WHAT ARE YOU DOING UP THERE?

I'M TAKING A SHORTCUT!

It takes just one minute to drive across West Virginia's New River Gorge Bridge. Before this arch bridge was built, people had to drive 40 minutes through mountains to cross the river.

The Chaotianmen Bridge is a road and rail bridge in China. **It is one of the longest arch bridges in the world.**

THAT'S A WHOLE LOT OF BRIDGE!

Cool Beams!

Have you ever walked across a log or wood plank when crossing a stream? That was a basic kind of beam bridge! While beam bridges are the simplest, most common type of bridge, engineers have still found ways to build them bigger and better. Some beam bridges need only two piers to support them, one at each end. Longer beam bridges are often strengthened by additional piers between the two ends. Beam bridges are brilliant!

Beam bridges with just two piers are built to cover short distances. This is because the farther apart a beam bridge's supports are, the weaker the bridge becomes.

THIS BRIDGE IS SO SHORT.

YEAH, BUT IT'S STRONG!

Modern beam bridges are built with steel beams called girders. The girders must hold up all the weight of the bridge.

Most highway bridges are beam bridges. They make it easy for us to drive from place to place.

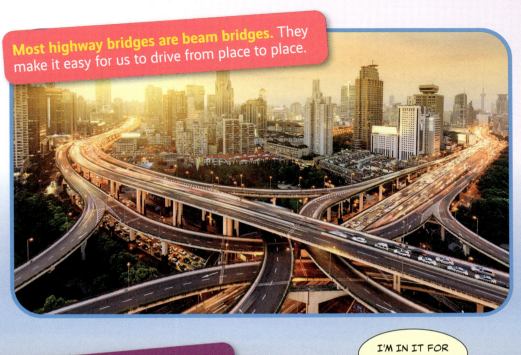

The world's longest beam bridge is the Lake Pontchartrain Causeway Bridge in Louisiana. It's 24 miles (39 km) long and runs completely over water!

For safety, the Causeway Bridge is made up of **thousands of separate sections that are each individually supported.**

I'M IN IT FOR THE LONG HAUL.

WHAT A LONG DRIVE! I HOPE THEY STOPPED FOR A BATHROOM BREAK FIRST!

In Suspense!

While beam bridges and arch bridges have been around since ancient times, a new style of bridge arrived on the scene in the 1800s—the modern suspension bridge. Since then, suspension bridges have become famous examples of excellent engineering. Using strong cables, these bridges can be built to span much longer distances than other types of bridges. Suspension bridges have changed bridge building forever!

The first modern suspension bridge was built in 1801 in Jacob's Creek, Pennsylvania.

Today's suspension bridges are built to withstand earthquakes. Metals used in their construction can bend during a quake, then straighten back into shape.

DID YOU FEEL THAT SHAKING? LET'S RUN AWAY!

NO WORRIES, THIS BRIDGE IS BUILT FOR IT.

To prove the Brooklyn Bridge's strength, famous circus showman P. T. Barnum marched 21 elephants across it!

The Great Golden Gate

One of the most famous—and spectacular—suspension bridges in the world is the Golden Gate Bridge. It was completed in 1937 after four years of construction. At that time, it was the world's longest suspension bridge. The bridge crosses the Golden Gate **Strait** near San Francisco, California. When thick fog from the Pacific Ocean rolls in, the Golden Gate Bridge's bright color comes in handy!

A Big Bridge Blunder

When bridges are built well, they can stand up against all kinds of weather and natural disasters, including earthquakes. But when their engineering is not quite right, they can fail—sometimes on a grand scale. That's what happened to Washington State's Tacoma Narrows Bridge, which collapsed just months after it opened in 1940. The doomed bridge's failure has gone down in history as one of the most famous bridge disasters ever. What went wrong?

As workers completed the bridge, they noticed something was wrong. **The bridge bounced up and down in strong winds, which earned it the nickname Galloping Gertie.**

A GALLOPING BRIDGE? THAT DOESN'T SEEM LIKE A GOOD THING!

LOOKS SCARY!

I FIND IT THRILLING! WOO-HOO!

As the bridge rolled in the wind, **thrill-seekers paid 75¢ to drive across it and 10¢ to cross on foot!**

The day it collapsed, the bridge twisted so much in the wind that **the sidewalk on one side was 28 ft (8.5 m) higher than the other side.**

COOL! LOOK AT THAT SIDEWALK RISING!

THIS BRIDGE IS COLLAPSING! I'M OUT OF HERE!

Luckily, no lives were lost during the bridge's dramatic collapse.

The bridge's famous collapse is one of the main reasons **model** structures of **large bridges are now tested in wind tunnels for safety.**

AND NOW I'M TRULY DONE FOR!

The bridge's remains are still at the bottom of Puget **Sound**. They form one of the world's largest human-made **reefs**.

Artsy Bridges

Bridges are all amazing in their own ways. While their main job is to help people travel more quickly and easily, some are so visually unique that they're considered works of art! From a bridge based on a rainbow to one in the form of a dragon, engineers have come up with some truly beautiful bridge designs. Let's take a look . . .

The Henderson Waves Bridge in Singapore looks like a huge, rolling wave of steel.

WHOEVER DESIGNED THIS WAS REALLY ON A ROLL!

Helix Bridge, also in Singapore, is shaped like a huge twisting spiral.

Gateshead Millennium Bridge is also called Winking Eye Bridge. This curved **pedestrian** bridge in England looks like—you guessed it—a winking eye!

HEY, DID THAT BRIDGE JUST WINK AT ME?

Gateshead Millennium Bridge can tilt up to allow boat traffic to pass beneath it.

Iran's Khaju Bridge was built around 1650. **Its 23 arches are beautifully decorated with tiles and paintings.**

In Vietnam, a bridge shaped like a dragon **shoots out fire.**

I'M ON FIRE!

23

Bridge MVPs

Looks aren't the only thing that can make a bridge stand out. There are bridges that can open their roadways, bridges built over ice, and even bridges that float! Many extraordinary bridges have been built all over the world. Here are some of the highlights . . .

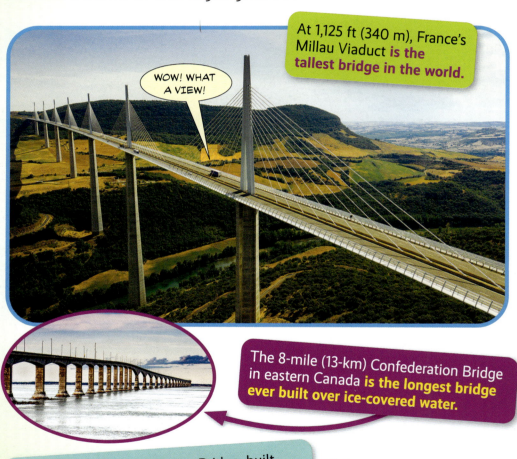

At 1,125 ft (340 m), France's Millau Viaduct **is the tallest bridge in the world.**

WOW! WHAT A VIEW!

The 8-mile (13-km) Confederation Bridge in eastern Canada **is the longest bridge ever built over ice-covered water.**

The Evergreen Point Floating Bridge, built across Lake Washington in Washington State, uses **pontoons** and anchors for support. **It's the longest floating bridge in the world.**

24

The Ponte Vecchio is the only stone arch bridge in Florence, Italy, that was not destroyed during World War II (1939–1945).

One of the most famous sights in London, England, is Tower Bridge, completed in 1894. Its roadway can be lifted open for boats to pass under it.

Sydney Harbor Bridge in Australia was built with about 58,200 tn. (52,800 t) of steel. That's a lot of metal!

Victoria Falls Bridge connects the countries of Zambia and Zimbabwe. It's a well-known spot to bungee jump!

A Bridge to the Future

From the bridges of ancient history to today's modern bridge marvels, people have long looked for better ways to build structures that connect places. Engineers are still working to make bridges stronger and safer. And advances in engineering will bring us even more amazing bridges in the future. Maybe you'll help build one of them someday!

The future of bridges may involve 3D printing! Amsterdam, Netherlands, is home to the world's first 3D-printed pedestrian bridge.

Since 3D printing builds something layer by layer, it uses only the materials that are needed. This means bridges can be made with very little construction waste.

In the future, people could go to more bridges for fun! **City parks may be built on top of bridges as a way to make the most of a city's space.**

FUTURE BRIDGES WILL BE COOL!

Engineers are finding new ways to build bridges that are less harmful to nature. In Singapore, pedestrian bridges were built 120 ft (36.5 m) over a forest to avoid disturbing the plants and animals there.

THANKS FOR HELPING!

NO PROBLEM!

Bridges of the future may have sensors to detect structural problems so they can be fixed. Now, that's smart!

Suspension Bridge
Craft Project

If you're an engineer who needs to design a bridge spanning thousands of feet over a body of water, you'd probably choose a suspension bridge. That style can span greater distances than any other type of bridge. Try your hand at building a long and strong bridge.

What You Will Need

- A piece of cardboard 17 x 11 inches (43 x 28 cm)
- Construction paper
- Scissors
- Glue
- 2 juice boxes
- A piece of thin cardboard 17 x 5 in. (43 x 13 cm)
- A black marker
- 4 paper tubes
- Tape
- String

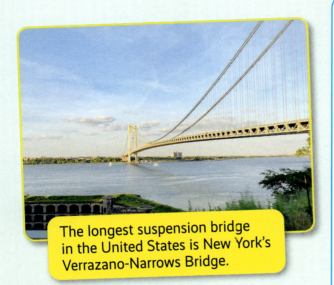

The longest suspension bridge in the United States is New York's Verrazano-Narrows Bridge.

The earliest suspension bridges were made of twisted grass! Hundreds of years ago, people used them to walk across spaces between cliffs.

Step One

Glue blue construction paper in the center of the cardboard. This is the river. Cut a piece of green construction paper in half. Glue the green paper on either side of the blue paper. Wrap the juice boxes in construction paper and glue a juice box in the center at each end of the cardboard. These are the piers of your bridge.

Step Two

Grab the piece of thin cardboard. Draw black dividing lines down the middle. Measure and mark the center point. Use scissors to cut two slits on each side of the center point. This is the bridge deck.

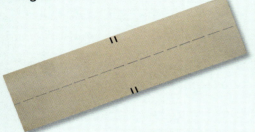

Step Three

Tape a paper tube to the cardboard base on each side of a pier. Repeat for the other pier. These are the support towers. Cut two slits at the top of each tube as shown in the photo.

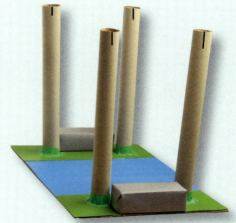

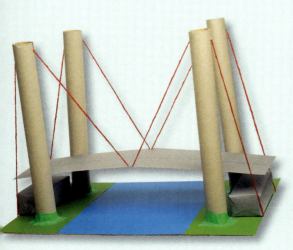

Step Four

Cut two pieces of string about 60 in. (152 cm) long. Position the bridge deck between the towers. Slip the center of one string through the slits on one side of the deck. Pull the string through the slits on the top of the towers. Then, tape the ends of the string in place on the bottom of the base, underneath the piers. Repeat on the other side of the deck.

Glossary

aqueducts structures built to carry water, often across valleys

cables strong ropes made of steel or fiber

concrete a hard material made from sand, gravel, cement, and water

deck the roadway or pathway of a bridge

engineering the practice of using science and math concepts to design things people use, such as bridges, roads, and dams

legend a story handed down from long ago that cannot be proven true or untrue

model a small copy of something, often used as a guide to make the thing in full size

pedestrian a person who is walking

piers heavy posts or pillars used to support a bridge or building

pontoons flat-bottomed boats used to support floating structures

reefs long structures that could naturally be formed from rock or coral at or near the surface of ocean waters

Renaissance an era of art, literature, and learning that began in Europe in the 1300s and lasted into the 1600s

sound a body of water between two larger bodies of water

span to extend across a space from end to end

strait a narrow body of water between two larger bodies of water

Read More

Dougherty, Rachel. *Secret Engineer: How Emily Roebling Built the Brooklyn Bridge*. New York: Roaring Brook Press, 2019.

McAneney, Caitie. *20 Fun Facts About Famous Bridges (Fun Fact File: Engineering Marvels)*. New York: Gareth Stevens Publishing, 2020.

Taylor, Charlotte and Melinda Farbman. *Bridges (Exploring Infrastructure)*. New York: Enslow Publishing, 2019.

Learn More Online

1. Go to **www.factsurfer.com** or scan the QR code below.

2. Enter "**X-Treme Bridges**" into the search box.

3. Click on the cover of this book to see a list of websites.

Index

ancient Romans 4, 10–12
aqueducts 10–12
arch bridges 6, 8, 12–13, 16, 23, 25
beam bridges 6, 14–16
Brooklyn Bridge 17
cables 7, 16
cable-stayed bridges 7
concrete 13
earthquakes 5, 16, 18, 20
Golden Gate Bridge 18–19
metal 6, 16, 25
parks 5, 27
piers 6, 12, 14, 29

Pont du Gard 10
Rialto Bridge 9
Roebling, Emily 17
ships 17
suspension bridges 6–7, 16–19, 28–29
Tacoma Narrows Bridge 20–21
truss bridges 6

About the Author

Catherine C. Finan is a writer living in northeastern Pennsylvania. She has just a *slight* case of gephyrophobia—the fear of crossing bridges!